SELF-MOTIVATION QUOTES FOR WOMEN

SELF-MOTIVATION QUOTES FOR WOMEN

Words of Wisdom to Empower and Inspire

BRIANA HOLLIS, LSW

ROCKRIDGE
PRESS

For general information on our other products and services or to obtain technical support, please contact our Customer Care Department within the United States at (866) 744-2665, or outside the United States at (510) 253-0500.

Rockridge Press publishes its books in a variety of electronic and print formats. Some content that appears in print may not be available in electronic books, and vice versa.

Interior and Cover Designer: Linda Snorina
Art Producer: Sara Feinstein
Production Editor: Jael Fogle
Production Manager: Jose Olivera

Illustration used under license from Creative Market.

Paperback ISBN: 978-1-63807-365-9
eBook ISBN: 978-1-63878-027-4
R0

INTRODUCTION

HI, I'M BRIANA! I'm so glad you picked up this book! Whether you're tired, busy, or a chronic procrastinator, motivation—or the lack thereof—is something that we all have to contend with from time to time.

Motivation can be intrinsic (from within) or extrinsic (from outside). Accomplishing a personal goal or doing something to simply make yourself happy is rooted in self-motivation, while wanting to impress someone or earn money is driven by external motivation. Many times, you'll find yourself having both intrinsic and extrinsic reasons for doing something. You may find your job incredibly rewarding personally and love the people that you work with, but you might find a new position if they cut your salary in half.

One of the times in my life when I needed the most motivation was when I was studying to become a social worker. Any course of study is difficult and becoming a social worker was no different. There were late nights, difficult clients (and colleagues), and times when I was ready to give up. However, I was self-motivated because of my goal of wanting to support others, and being a social worker was the way that I wanted to do it. I could see myself being of service to others and that was a goal I wasn't going to quit on.

Both types of motivation can be useful and necessary; however, if you don't have self-motivation, you may find that it is a lot harder to get things done. For example, if you live alone, no one is going to make you wash the dishes—believe me, I've been waiting. Self-motivation will help drive you when there is no one else around to help push you forward or when there are no external rewards.

The quotes and stories in this book are to help you spark that self-motivation. The incredible people documented in this book have done amazing things that we can all learn from. There's no need to read this book cover to cover. You can jump around to the quotes and stories that resonate the most with you.

I mentioned that I'm a chronic procrastinator. I don't mean to be but sometimes life gets in the way. Or sometimes I may just want to lie in bed and watch the latest Netflix drama. I may even be procrastinating on writing this book right now. Sorry if that happens! Just kidding, if you're reading this book, it didn't happen. If, like me, you're a chronic procrastinator, or otherwise need some motivation, let the accomplished women in this book give you the extra boost you need to get it all done!

We just need to be kinder to ourselves. If we treated ourselves the way we treated our best friend, can you imagine how much better off we would be?

—MEGHAN MARKLE

Spend less time tearing yourself apart, worrying if you're good enough. You are good enough. And you're going to meet amazing people in your life who will help you and love you.

—REESE WITHERSPOON

If you're comfortable with yourself and know yourself, you're going to shine and radiate, and other people are going to be drawn to you.

—DOLLY PARTON

I'm a believer in the power of knowledge and the ferocity of beauty, so from my point of view, your life is already artful—waiting, just waiting, for you to make it art.

—TONI MORRISON

Do not edit your desires.
We are entitled to ambition.
We are entitled to success.
We are entitled to failure. And any
moment of compromise on those
three things starts to weaken
who we are.

—STACEY ABRAMS

Society tries to define us and tries to limit us. So I would say, do not listen to that, ignore all of that, and believe in yourself.

—MALALA YOUSAFZAI

Keep chasing those moments where you discover something new about your voice. Don't ever let that end. Keep your minds and hearts open to life's endless and unforeseeable possibilities.

—OCTAVIA SPENCER

Don't ever underestimate the importance you can have because history has shown us that courage can be contagious and hope can take on a life of its own.

—MICHELLE OBAMA

You have to have insane confidence in yourself, even if it's not real. . . . I'm giving you permission to root for yourself. And while you're at it, root for those around you, too.

—MINDY KALING

A joyful woman, by merely being, says it all. The world is terrified of joyful women. Make a stand. Be one anyway.

—MARIANNE WILLIAMSON

VICTORIA CRUZ didn't know that she'd be at the beginning of a movement when she went to the Stonewall Inn on June 27, 1969. The Stonewall Riot happened that night and ignited her spark to advocate for the LGBTQ+ community. Everything that she does for LGBTQ+ individuals, she does because she believes in keeping the community together. From participating in the first Pride March in history to working with the Anti-Violence Project, Cruz understands that there will be both progress and bumps along the road to equality. Even though the LGBTQ+ community continues to struggle, she believes the future is bigger and brighter than could be imagined.

Finally, I was able to see that if I had a contribution I wanted to make, I must do it, despite what others said. That I was okay the way I was. That it was all right to be strong.

—WANGARI MAATHAI

It makes me feel very strongly that, as women, we need to fight for support systems. We need to be activists; women need to be in decision-making roles.

—DOLORES HUERTA

I'm optimistic and I'm hopeful that it will change for the better. There's power in numbers. If we unite and keep united, we can make the future different.

—VICTORIA CRUZ

When one door of happiness

closes, another opens;

but often we look so long

at the closed door that

we do not see the one which

has been opened for us.

—HELEN KELLER

The thing that is really hard, and really amazing, is giving up on being perfect and beginning the work of becoming yourself.

—ANNA QUINDLEN

And the most valuable characteristic any would-be writer can possibly have is persistence. Just keep at it, keep learning your craft and keep trying.

—OCTAVIA BUTLER

You have as much right as anyone else to be in this world, and to be in any profession you want . . . You don't have to wait for permission.

—MAE JEMISON

Your emotions make you human. Even the unpleasant ones have a purpose. Don't lock them away. If you ignore them, they just get louder and angrier.

—SABAA TAHIR

I've been like this my whole life and I embrace me. I love how I look. I am a full woman and I'm strong, and I'm powerful, and I'm beautiful at the same time.

—SERENA WILLIAMS

27

I don't need to have to care so much about what other people think, because the people that are going to be kind and sweet and support me are the true people, true friends.

—MING-NA WEN

Though she was already quite accomplished, being both a physician and engineer, **MAE JEMISON** dreamed of going to space one day. Inspired by Sally Ride, the first woman in space and Nichelle Nichols, the actress who played Lieutenant Uhura on *Star Trek*, she made her dream a reality. When she applied to the astronaut training program, she was 1 of only 15 people accepted, becoming the first Black woman in the program. Less than 10 years later, she became the first Black woman in space on the shuttle *Endeavour* on September 12, 1992. As a woman who completed many "firsts," Jemison shows that representation is important and that women have so much to contribute if only given the chance.

I made my first film when
I was 35, so I firmly believe
that you don't have to be one
thing in life. If you're doing
something, and you have
a desire to do something
different, give it a try.

—AVA DUVERNAY

The people who have been unaware are now starting to wake up, and once we become aware, we change. We can change and people are ready for change.

—GRETA THUNBERG

Someone, somewhere, will say,
"Don't do it. You don't have what
it takes to survive the wilderness."
This is when you reach deep into
your wild heart and remind yourself,
"I *am* the wilderness."

—BRENÉ BROWN

I have come to believe over and over again that what is most important to me must be spoken, made verbal and shared, even at the risk of having it bruised or misunderstood.

—AUDRE LORDE

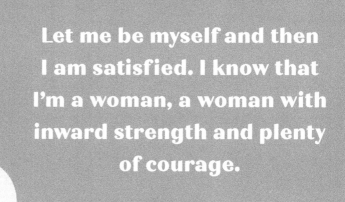

Let me be myself and then I am satisfied. I know that I'm a woman, a woman with inward strength and plenty of courage.

—ANNE FRANK

I say no to my own instinct to stay quiet. It's a way of kicking down the boundaries that society has set up for women—be compliant, be a caregiver, be quiet—and erecting my own.

—LINDY WEST

We bring a deeper commitment
to our happiness when we
fully understand that our time
left is limited and we really
need to make it count.

—ELISABETH KÜBLER-ROSS

Your life is your story, and the adventure ahead of you is the journey to fulfill your own purpose and potential.

—KERRY WASHINGTON

I no longer choose to believe in old limitations and lack, I now choose to begin to see myself as the Universe sees me—perfect, whole, and complete.

—LOUISE HAY

It's all okay. Just keep showing up, and keep offering yourself compassion. Little by little, the work will get done.

—LEE CHAIX MCDONOUGH

MARIE KONDO leapt into our collective consciousness through her book *The Life-Changing Magic of Tidying Up*. In this book, Kondo spread the message that the key to getting organized was finding joy in the things you owned. If an item "sparks joy," keep it and continue to allow that joy into your life. If it doesn't, let it go so that it can bring joy to someone else. Kondo believes that joy can be either fleeting or long-lasting, and that both types of joy serve an important purpose. For Kondo, joy is personal and depends on creating your own definition. The message of "sparking joy" is powerful and can connect us to what truly matters and grounds us in why we do what we do and why we have what we have.

I just want everybody to feel you can do something if you feel ready for it. Don't rely on somebody else telling you that.

—JASMINE HARRISON

Unless these things get spoken about and get showcased, you never get to realize the opportunities that are around the corner.

—KATE MIDDLETON

I don't have to prove anything to anyone. I only have to follow my heart and concentrate on what I want to say to the world. I run my world.

—BEYONCÉ

The process is to look at what sparks joy in your life, say goodbye to the objects that don't, and be grateful for the ones you decide to keep.

—MARIE KONDO

It's so important just to be true to yourself and to own your own character and take responsibility for it, and speak up and say, "This isn't right; this isn't me."

—BECKY LYNCH

I just love bossy women.
I could be around them all day.
To me, bossy is not a pejorative
term at all. It means somebody's
passionate and engaged
and ambitious and doesn't
mind leading.

—AMY POEHLER

It took me quite a long time to develop a voice, and now that I have it, I am not going to be silent.

—MADELEINE ALBRIGHT

*Dream with ambition,
lead with conviction, and see
yourself in a way that others
might not see you, simply
because they've never seen it
before. And we will applaud
you every step of the way.*

—KAMALA HARRIS

People often talk about how I'm courageous, but I believe everybody should be courageous. Courage is being scared to death but remaining resolute.

—ILHAN OMAR

I am not lucky. You know what I am? I am smart, I am talented, I take advantage of the opportunities that come my way and I work really, really hard.

—SHONDA RHIMES

LAVERNE COX went from being bullied as a young person to being a trailblazing actress and activist for LGBTQ+ rights. By being exactly who she is, she became the first transgender person to be nominated for an Emmy and to be featured on the cover of *Time*. She understands that her presence makes an impact on the communities in which she belongs. In her work as both an activist and actress, Cox strives to maintain professional vulnerability but also takes the time to take care of herself. She possesses deep empathy and compassion, which brings her to fight for the inclusion of marginalized people. She wants to continue to elevate the voices of those who continue to struggle and ensure that diverse voices are in the rooms where decisions are being made. Cox owns her story and prompts all of us to own ours.

There's too much to be done. There are too many people who need help. Someone has to do the work and set the example, so why not me?

—INDIA WALTON

People, I think, mistake that it's just winning. Sometimes it could be, but for me it's hitting the best sets I can, gaining confidence and having a good time and having fun.

—SIMONE BILES

If any female feels she need anything beyond herself to legitimate and validate her existence, she is already giving away her power to be self-defining, her agency.

—bell hooks

A lot of what feminism is about is moving outside of roles and moving outside of expectations of who and what you're supposed to be to live a more authentic life.

—LAVERNE COX

My mantra, my favorite, favorite, favorite thing is, "The privilege of a lifetime is being who you are." That you are the event. I love it. I feel like it says it all.

—VIOLA DAVIS

I am inviting you to step forward, to be seen. And to ask yourself, if not me, who? If not now, when?

—EMMA WATSON

I've given myself the gift of compassion because I was able to look at so many other women, I was able to take some of that and put it back on myself.

—STACY LONDON

Life comes with many challenges. The ones that should not scare us are the ones we can take on and take control of.

—ANGELINA JOLIE

I felt such a relief in that moment and free enough from the demon that was my self-doubt, that I could actually go away and do the work.

—LUPITA NYONG'O

I know my worth. I embrace my power. I say if I'm beautiful. I say if I'm strong. You will not determine my story. I will.

—AMY SCHUMER

JAZZ JENNINGS has never been shy about sharing her story. She came into the spotlight when she was interviewed by Barbara Walters about her transition at just six years old. Since then, Jazz has shared about being a transgender teen to anyone who was willing to listen. Not only has she been interviewed numerous times, her show, *I Am Jazz*, provides an intimate look at what it is like being a transgender teen. Jazz describes that there were times when she felt trapped in her body and believes that everyone should be able to love their bodies. Because this journey can be so difficult for trans youth, she wants to pave the way for them. She says that she will continue her advocacy, including all who demand equality, because "the world needs some changing."

Here's my short version: if you're going to speak truth to power, make sure it's the truth. That's a good maxim.

—MARGARET ATWOOD

[The goal] should be to create meaning by getting as close to the truth as possible in everything you do, whether it's a character you play, the choices you make.

—CONSTANCE WU

I believe in glorifying all bodies. All of them. Because every single person in the entire world deserves to feel good about and love themselves. It's that simple.

—JES BAKER

So I chose to tell myself a different story from the one women are told. I decided I was safe. I was strong. I was brave. Nothing could vanquish me.

—CHERYL STRAYED

It also takes our team leaders being willing to speak up and say things that are uncomfortable. When one person does that, they give permission to others to do the same.

—JORDYN WIEBER

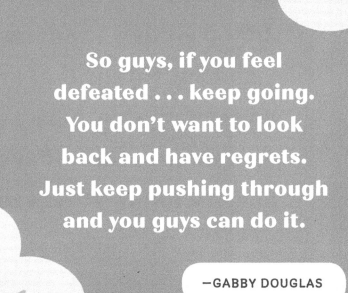

So guys, if you feel defeated . . . keep going. You don't want to look back and have regrets. Just keep pushing through and you guys can do it.

—GABBY DOUGLAS

Once you realize that your consciousness is all that matters— your thoughts and experiences truly shape who you are—then the physical characteristics don't matter anymore.

—JAZZ JENNINGS

You only have so much time or energy, you start channeling it into the things that matter to you and the people that matter to you.

—SOPHIA DI MARTINO

All of us are put in boxes by our family, by our religion, by our society, our moment in history, even our own bodies. Some people have the courage to break free.

—GEENA ROCERO

I don't really have a word for myself, or a category that I put myself in. I don't think about it too much, I just wear what feels good.

—SAMIRA WILEY

ELIZABETH GILBERT rose to prominence with the release of her memoir *Eat, Pray, Love* in 2006. In the wake of a devastating divorce, Gilbert traveled the world and found herself there, too. One principle from those days of traveling light remained with her long after her experience: that of always removing something from her pack to admit one new item. In deciding what should stay, she had to choose things to support her every single day. Applying this principle to life would allow her to create a life that looked like hers—not anyone else's—and honor the most accurate parts of herself. Her book *Big Magic* centers on helping others create a life that allows them a joyful spirit.

I think growing up in a world where it's so hard to be understood and heard in the right way, I've learned the importance of having self-love and self-confidence.

—HAILEE STEINFELD

I have never been insecure,
ever, about how I look,
about what I want to do with
myself. My mum told me
to only ever do things for
myself, not for others.

—ADELE

You fight for it, strive for it,
insist upon it, and sometimes even
travel around the world looking
for it. You have to participate
relentlessly in the manifestations
of your own blessings.

—ELIZABETH GILBERT

People often say that "beauty is in the eye of the beholder," and I say that the most liberating thing about beauty is realizing that you are the beholder.

—SALMA HAYEK

*And, by the way,
to me self-care does not mean
going to the spa. It's learning to
say no. It's knowing yourself so
you can make choices that are
an expression of you.
That's self-care.*

—TRACEE ELLIS ROSS

Power for me is "no." . . . That's when you know your worth, when you know your value. And that's power for me.

—TARAJI P. HENSON

I'm all about body positivity and self-love because I believe that we can save the world if we first save ourselves.

—LIZZO

It wasn't really until my mid-thirties that I started to feel confident or feel a flame: the power of my individual self. I had started to see the beauty and the power of other individuals.

—KATHRYN HAHN

It's all about encouragement. Everyone knows that a compliment goes a very long way, and you never know what someone's going through in their life—giving them a compliment might mean the world to them.

—GIGI GORGEOUS

And one day we'll all be like that. These moments are all part of being a human being. So, this tapestry of images is about trying to show everybody as dignified and beautiful.

—SHIRIN NESHAT

Thirty-five years into her career, **REGINA KING** is now being recognized for her phenomenal talent. She's an award-winning actress, director, and producer. Her film directorial debut was *One Night in Miami*, a film that showcases the dreams and ambitions of four famous Black men. In this film, she used her artistic voice to express a reality that is not often seen. When asked how she does it all, she states that it comes from loving what she does and being willing to work hard at it. King also recognizes that what might work for her, may not work for someone else. She believes that everyone should do whatever is successful for them and be willing to take a risk.

If you just do you and remain true to yourself, then you don't really need validation from anybody. So, I think it comes down to self-love and taking care of yourself before anything else.

—MARSAI MARTIN

To be able to raise your voice and say something is physicalizing the first act of what it is to declare your space, and your personhood in a crowd of people.

—SANDRA OH

It starts with education, advocacy, and being there for your loved ones and for yourself. By giving, you receive. By giving yourself, a funny thing happens: you receive some comfort also.

—ANGELA BASSETT

You want real and you want powerful so that girls can realize, "I can relate to it," or something truthful, but [they] could also aspire to it. Like "I could be her."

—DANAI GURIRA

I am on an upward trajectory.
A lot of this I'm discovering
along the way, but I am not
compromising my integrity.
I'm always continuing
to dream.

—REGINA KING

It emboldens folks, and you realize you have support and you're not squeaking just on your own behalf. You're squeaking for everybody.

—TESSA THOMPSON

And there are a bunch of women at the center of it—strong women, flawed women. Any day you employ women, to me, is a good day.

—BLAKE LIVELY

And, in the good times, really embrace and enjoy them. Beforehand I'd be like, "What's next? What's next? What's next?" instead of appreciating being in the moment.

—RAVEN SAUNDERS

There's so many dimensions to a woman and I believe, for me, this is a departure from the girl. I love the girl that lives in me. I love her, but this Woman has overpowered her.

—JILL SCOTT

We gotta say the things we want to say. We gotta write the things we want to write. We need to connect with the people that we want to connect with.

—PHILLIPA SOO

After hitting the lowest point in her life, **MANDY MARTINI CHIHUAILAF** found strength and hope through leaning into ancestral knowledge. Chihuailaf is both a teacher and writer who supports others in their healing journey by reclaiming what wellness is. She believes that healing is deeply personal and that healing comes from being reunited with ourselves and nature. Nature speaks to us, but many of us have not been taught how to listen. Chihuailaf believes that we must learn to question what we've been taught and to seek new perspectives. Chihuailaf teaches that by reuniting with this sacred knowledge, we can heal ourselves, one another, and the earth itself.

I don't think that success is linear. I think that it's going to be ups and downs on the way to those goals but encouraging everybody to challenge themselves to see how high their elevator can go.

—SKYLAR DIGGINS-SMITH

One day you will appreciate the upgrade of that cruise control but never take your eye off that winding road you have paved by being courageously you!

—CHRISSY METZ

This is my charge to everybody: Do what you can. Do what you have to do. Step outside of yourself. Be more. Be better. Be bigger than you've ever been before.

—MEGAN RAPINOE

What I have found is that there's love to be found. There's joy there. There's suffering. There's redemption. All of it. And that's what it means to be human.

—MICHELLE ALEXANDER

Do something and fail. See what happens. The world will not end. You will not stop breathing. Your friends will not abandon you. You'll conquer your fears only by experiencing them.

—ANGELA DUCKWORTH

[When men determine who is a heroine] this perpetuates the difficulties that all women experience when we have to self-validate. We don't need a man to say, "You are an extraordinary woman!"

—PHILIPPA GREGORY

That's how we connect,
and that's a state of us being,
that's how we're reminded
every day of what we're a part
of. Listening is healing,
and healing ourselves is
healing the land.

—MANDY MARTINI CHIHUAILAF

Failure isn't the opposite of success, but a stepping stone to success. And . . . fearlessness is not the absence of fear, but the mastery of fear.

—ARIANNA HUFFINGTON

So we pursue in reality the things that we're capable of imagining, and those of us who are in industries or fields that play with imagination have a responsibility to depict futures that are for everyone.

—N. K. JEMISIN

It was always about what others thought about my body, until I gained a voice. Now I get to tell people what I think of my body.

—ASHLEY GRAHAM

BOLA SOKUNBI is a certified financial educator who made her own financial mistakes and wants other women to know that they are not alone in that. Clever Girl Finance grew out of Sokunbi's mission to help women take charge of their finances and live life on their own terms. Sokunbi believes that knowledge is power and there are more options available for women than they realize. Her mother, whom she deemed the "hustle queen," showed her the importance of financial education and empowerment for women. To Sokunbi, building wealth and having financial peace of mind is available for everyone, even if there are roadblocks on the journey there.

I have agency. I am comfortable with who I am. I know my voice. I know what I want to say to the world.

—GABOUREY SIDIBE

My passion for this position revolves around getting more money into the hands of women. When women have more money, they have more power—and then good things happen to society.

—SALLIE KRAWCHECK

You really gotta be about the action if you're going to do it. If there's a real way to tangibly help the things we talk about, let's do it, in real life.

—AARON ROSE PHILIP

What you don't know can become your greatest asset if you'll let it and if you have the confidence to say, "I'm going to do it anyway."

—SARA BLAKELY

Every person has their own story, their own struggle that they came through, and they are still pushing towards their dreams and they continued to dream even after losing a lot.

—YUSRA MARDINI

As a woman making strides with my finances, I can set the example for my daughter. I can show her how not to let other people use her gender as a limitation.

—BOLA SOKUNBI

You're not alone with your experiences and your feelings. It can really be helpful sometimes to hear somebody else say the thing out loud that you were struggling with.

—DR. JOY HARDEN BRADFORD

We are beginning to discover the power of accepting how you feel. The power of saying even though I am anxious, I honor how I feel, I accept these feelings.

—JESSICA ORTNER

There is so much hope in young people, and when I say young people, I do mean myself— people my own age—but I also mean younger.

—ZENDAYA

I feel like I have a responsibility to change that narrative for myself, for other people who look like me, and really for anyone who hasn't seen themselves represented.

—DEEPICA MUTYALA

DR. JOY HARDEN BRADFORD founded Therapy for Black Girls as a blog in 2014 after watching *Black Girls Rock!* on BET. Therapy for Black Girls eventually grew into a directory for women to find therapists and a successful podcast. Harden Bradford uses her platform to eradicate mental health stigma, especially in the Black community, and to speak to the numerous benefits therapy can provide. She recounts that many people have a mistrust of the mental health system and prefer to keep their problems within their household. Her hope is that her voice can help others find the courage to take advantage of therapy with a therapist whom they can trust and with whom they can build a relationship.

In my head, I was like "you could do this and that and this and that . . ." That was a sign to me that I might be more ready than I thought.

—LISA LUCAS

When you see someone
like you doing something,
I think it lights a fire inside
you that makes you think,
"I can do that too!"

—NYMA TANG

We are at a tough time, but I believe that it's possible to really activate what I like to call our liberatory imaginations to what it is that will deeply bring us joy.

—SONYA RENEE TAYLOR

I feel very empowered by my own history. The life I've lived, the lives of my friends. I want to honor them. I want to honor everything that made me what I am.

—MICHAELA COEL

You don't have to know anything. You learn as you go. You can write your plans to the finest detail, but you really don't start until you start. Trust yourself. You'll be okay.

—JENI BRITTON BAUER

Do your best at all times and make it as correct as possible. Work as if someone is watching you. Then you'll be prepared when an opportunity presents itself.

—KATHERINE JOHNSON

*When you come
out of your own hard times,
trials and tribulations, people
look up to you for guidance,
and to show them a path
to help them overcome
their own hurdles.*

—HARNAAM KAUR

My philosophy has always been that life isn't about what you don't have. It's about what you do with the gifts that you're given.

—TATYANA MCFADDEN

But we have a multitude of identities—there's pride in being a woman, there's pride in being Black, and there's pride in being disabled.

—MAMA CAX

No matter what age you are, your voice should be heard and you can develop a passion for something and be an activist in your own right.

—ISKRA LAWRENCE

HARNAAM KAUR lives by the phrase "my body, my rules." She is known for her beautiful beard, and being the youngest woman in the world with a full beard. The body confidence activist and self-love advocate hasn't always been confident in her body. Kaur had surprising physical changes when she entered into her teen years, which included weight gain and growing facial hair. This resulted in being diagnosed with polycystic ovarian syndrome at 12 years old. She was bullied and discriminated against but chose to be authentically herself. Growing out her beard at sixteen, she has since spoken out about bullying, confidence, and body positivity. Kaur is breaking stereotypes about what women look like and providing young women guidance and support.

[She's] going to have to be very strategic to get what [she wants]. That this is bigger than she would ever dream of, but that it is possible. And that's magical.

—JILLIAN MERCADO

I know the value of helping a person when they have no hope. I'm a walking reminder of that. All the help I was given in my life made me the person I am.

—NADIA NADIM

I would say whatever your dream is to keep pushing for it, no matter what it is or what people think about it. If it's your dream, never settle.

—WINNIE HARLOW

Why should anyone make me feel this is what I should do? Why? Whatever path you go down, you should feel comfortable with it.

—ENYA

I hope that by living authentically and unapologetically, I can inspire others to have the courage to utilize their voice to its fullest potential—to make change.

—HONEY DIJON

But the experiences that I have with each of these identities has made me who I am today and has given me the strength to live in my truth.

—RAHNE JONES

For me to have grace is to be seen as a human being that gets to be flawed, gets to be misunderstood, and hopefully, still deserves love.

—INDYA MOORE

That was like a lifeline for me internally. It was like, there's something here, there is energy here. I can keep putting energy into this, and it keeps feeding me.

—CHANI NICHOLAS

We have to give ourselves permission, no matter what's going on around us, to say that our mental health is important. It doesn't matter what your friends or family or culture says.

—DR. ALFIEE BRELAND-NOBLE

Not trying to avoid the hardness and the painfulness that can come from vulnerability. There's no need to run from it. Because from that space of tender vulnerability, that's where flowers bloom.

—JESSAMYN STANLEY

REFERENCES

Aggeler, Madeleine. "Taraji P. Henson on Being a Single Mom, Loving the Word 'No' and Getting Paid." The Cut, October 16, 2017. TheCut.com/2017/10/taraji-p-henson -loves-the-word-no.html.

Alexander, Kerri Lee. "Mae Jemison." National Women's History Museum. Accessed August 12, 2021. WomensHistory.org/education-resources/biographies /mae-jemison.

American Foundation for the Blind. "Helen Keller Quotes on Happiness." Accessed August 7, 2021. AFB.org/about-afb/history/helen-keller/helen-keller-quotes /helen-keller-quotes-happiness.

Artavia, David. "Stonewall Survivor Victoria Cruz on the Future of the LGBTQ Movement." *Advocate*. June 18, 2019. Advocate.com/exclusives/2019/6/18 /stonewall-survivor-victoria-cruz-future-lgbtq-movement.

Axon, Rachel. "Simone Biles Doesn't Let Expectations Overwhelm Her." *USA Today*. June 3, 2016. USAToday.com/story/sports/olympics/rio-2016/2016/06/02 /simone-biles-expectations-rio/85298782.

Baker, Jes. *Things No One Will Tell Fat Girls: A Handbook for Unapologetic Living*. Berkeley, CA: Seal Press, 2015.

Beard, Alison. "Life's Work: An Interview with Marie Kondo." *Harvard Business Review*, April 14, 2020. HBR.org/2020/05/lifes-work-an-interview-with-marie-kondo.

Bencomo Lobaco, Julia. "Dolores Huerta: The Vision and Voice of Her Life's Work." AARP. 2004. AARP.org/politics-society/history/info-2004/interview_dolores _hurerta.html.

Betker, Ally. "Model-Activist Mama Cax on Traveling with a Disability." *Here Magazine*. Accessed August 8, 2021. HereMagazine.com/articles/mama-cax-packing-list.

Biography.com. "Mae C. Jemison." July 15, 2021. Biography.com/astronaut/mae-c -jemison.

Birch, Jenna. "Inside Jeni's Splendid Ice Creams' Scrappy Climb to the Top." The Helm, May 21, 2020. TheHelm.co/jenis-splendid-ice-creams-founder-jeni-britton-bauer -interview.

Brown, Jera. "The WD Interview: Author N. K. Jemisin on Creating New Worlds and Playing with Imagination." *Writer's Digest*, March 29, 2019. WritersDigest.com/be -inspired/the-wd-interview-n-k-jemisin.

Calaor, Jesa Marie. "Jazz Jennings on Overcoming Insecurities: 'Your Thoughts and Experiences Shape Who You Are.'" POPSUGAR Beauty, June 15, 2019. PopSugar .com/beauty/photo-gallery/46245256/image/46246659/Jazz-Jennings -Overcoming-Her-Insecurities.

Cave, Rosie. "On Beauty: Winnie Harlow." *British Vogue*, August 16, 2017. Vogue.co.uk /article/winnie-harlow-beauty-interview.

Charuza, Nikita. "Why Deepica Mutyala's Live Tinted Products Are for 'Every Shade in Between.'" POPSUGAR Beauty, September 2, 2020. PopSugar.com/beauty /deepica-mutyala-live-tinted-interview-47747640?stream_view=1#photo -47747646.

Chew-Bose, Durga. "Michaela Coel's Pressure Points." Garage, September 10, 2020. Garage.Vice.com/en_us/article/7kpajz/michaela-coel-garage-liz-johnson-artur.

Chia, Jessica. "Ashley Graham Is Tired of Being Told How to Feel about Her Body." *Allure*, June 18, 2019. Allure.com/story/ashley-graham-cover-interview-2019.

citytvofficial. "'Suits' Star Meghan Markle Talks International Day of the Girl." YouTube, October 7, 2015. YouTube.com/watch?v=Ape4M6jXw0s.

Clever Girl Finance. "Meet Bola Sokunbi." Accessed August 12, 2021. CleverGirlFinance.com/about-bola.

Couric, Katie. "Amy Poehler Tells Katie Couric, 'I Just Love Bossy Women!'" *Glamour*, March 28, 2011. Glamour.com/story/amy-poehler-tells-katie-couric-i-just-love-bossy-women.

Crumpton, Taylor. "We Asked Black Queer Icons to Share Their Dreams for the Future." them, February 28, 2020. Them.us/story/we-asked-black-queer-icons-to-share-their-dreams-for-the-future.

CUNY Academic Commons. "Lorde, the Transformation of Silence into Language and Action." WGS10016. Accessed August 7, 2021. wgs10016.commons.gc.CUNY.edu/lorde-poetry-is-not-a-luxury.

Daily Mail. "Adele: 'I Have All The Say; I Have Power over Everything I Do.'" February 13, 2009. DailyMail.co.uk/home/you/article-1135182/Adele-I-say-I-power-I-do.html.

Dartmouth. "2018 Commencement Address by Mindy Kaling '01." June 10, 2018. home.Dartmouth.edu/news/2018/06/2018-commencement-address-mindy-kaling-01.

Davies, Paul. "29 of Greta Thunberg's Best Quotes—Curious Earth: Climate Change." *Curious Earth* (blog), April 14, 2021. curious.earth/blog/greta-thunberg-quotes-best-21.

"Detroit's Fashion Speak & My Interview with Stacy London." Haneen's Haven, October 23, 2017. Haneens-Haven.com/detroits-fashion-speak-my-interview-with-stacy-london-d96.

Dr. Joy. "Biography." Accessed August 12, 2021. HelloDrJoy.com/about.

Elizabeth Gilbert. "Bio." Accessed August 13, 2021. ElizabethGilbert.com/bio.

Elle. "Zendaya and Timothée Talk 'Euphoria' Season 2, 'Malcom and Marie,' and Her Historic Emmy Win." December 8, 2020. HeadTopics.com/us/zendaya-and-timothee-talk-euphoria-season-2-malcom-and-marie-and-her-historic-emmy-win-17315569.

Elle. "Zendaya Is the Best Thing to Happen to Hollywood." November 10, 2020. Elle.com/culture/a34601455/zendaya-euphoria-dune-interview.

Epstein, Rachel. "Raven Saunders Is Getting Another Shot at Life—and the Gold." *Marie Claire*, July 23, 2021. MarieClaire.com/health-fitness/a37022973/raven-saunders-tokyo-olympics-interview-2021.

ESPN.com. "Becky Lynch's improbable journey to WWE stardom." September 22, 2016. ESPN.com/wwe/story/_/id/17611954/becky-lynch-says-everybody-knows-four-horsewomen-deserve-main-event-wrestlemania.

Eyewitness News ABC7NY. "Megan Rapinoe's Full World Cup Parade Speech." YouTube, July 10, 2019. YouTube.com/watch?v=jDrB2IestHs&t=2s&ab_channel=EyewitnessNewsABC7NY.

Faith, Paloma. "Sophia Di Martino, with Some Help from Paloma Faith, Looks Back on *Loki*." *Interview Magazine*, July 22, 2021. InterviewMagazine.com/culture/sophia-di-martino-paloma-faith-looks-back-on-loki.

Feller, Madison. "India Walton on Running to Be Buffalo's First Female Mayor: 'I Don't Have Room in My Spirit for Fear.'" *Elle*, July 8, 2021. Elle.com/culture/career-politics/a36957732/india-walton-buffalo-first-female-mayor-campaign-interview.

Frank, Robert. "Billionaire Sara Blakely Says Secret to Success Is Failure." CNBC, October 16, 2013. CNBC.com/2013/10/16/billionaire-sara-blakely-says-secret-to-success-is-failure.html.

Gay, Roxane. "The Talented Tessa Thompson." *Town & Country*, January 15, 2021. TownAndCountryMag.com/leisure/arts-and-culture/a35031662/tessa-thompson -sylvies-love-roxane-gay-interview.

Gilbert, Elizabeth. *Big Magic: Creative Living beyond Fear*. New York: Riverhead Books, 2016.

Gilbert, Elizabeth. *Eat, Pray, Love: One Woman's Search for Everything across Italy, India and Indonesia*. New York: Riverhead Books, 2016.

Glamour. "*Glamour*'s January Cover Star Reese Witherspoon on Her Biggest Fears (in Real Life and in Her New Film *Wild*)." December 2, 2014. Glamour.com/story /reese-witherspoon-glamour-cover.

Guardian. "Anne Frank: 10 Beautiful Quotes from *The Diary of a Young Girl*." January 27, 2015. TheGuardian.com/childrens-books-site/2015/jan/27/the-greatest-anne -frank-quotes-ever.

Harris, Hunter. "Regina King, Long May She Reign." *InStyle*, January 6, 2021. InStyle.com/celebrity/regina-king-february-cover.

Haskell, Rob. "At 45, Tracee Ellis Ross Is Living Her Best Life." InStyle.com, October 3, 2018. InStyle.com/news/tracee-ellis-ross-november-cover.

Hay, Louise L. *You Can Heal Your Life*. Alexandria, NSW: Hay House, Inc., 2015.

hooks, bell. *Feminism Is for Everybody: Passionate Politics*. Brooklyn, NY: South End Press, 2000.

Horne, Karama. "Danai Gurira on Black Female Agency in *Black Panther*." SYFY, February 16, 2018. SYFY.com/syfywire/danai-gurira-on-black-female-agency-in -black-panther. [Article no longer on the website.]

Iman and Tia Williams. *The Beauty of Color: The Ultimate Beauty Guide for Skin of Color*. New York: Putnam, 2005. Foreword by Salma Hayek, p. 1.

Industrial Scripts. "15 Inspiring Ava DuVernay Quotes for Writers & Filmmakers." September 9, 2019. IndustrialScripts.com/ava-duvernay-quotes.

Jackson, Jada. "Meet Hollywood's Youngest Producer." Coveteur, accessed August 1, 2021. Coveteur.com/marsai-martin.

Jairke Robbins. "The Tapping Solution: Interview with Jessica Ortner." Accessed August 8, 2021. JairekRobbins.com/the-tapping-solution-interview-with-jessica-ortner.

Jary, Marta. "Lizzo Explains Why She Preaches 'Body Positivity' after Jillian Michaels Comments about Her Weight." Daily Mail Online, January 12, 2020. DailyMail.co.uk/tvshowbiz/article-7878189/Lizzo-explains-preaches-body-positivity-Jillian-Michaels-comments-weight.html.

Jensen, Kelly. *Here We Are: Feminism for the Real World*. Chapel Hill, NC: Algonquin, 2017.

Jolie, Angelina. "My Medical Choice." *New York Times*, May 14, 2013. NYTimes.com/2013/05/14/opinion/my-medical-choice.html.

Jones Jr., Robert. "Thank You for Everything, Victoria Cruz." Brooklyn College, June 17, 2019. Brooklyn.CUNY.edu/web/news/bcstories/thank-you-for-everything-victoria-cruz.php.

Kaur, Harnaam. "Harnaam Kaur: 'How I Learned to Love My Facial Hair and Use My Experience as a Force for Good in the World.'" *Glamour UK*, September 17, 2018. GlamourMagazine.co.uk/article/harnaam-kaur-online-bullying-interview.

Khaleeli, Homa. "The Lady with a Beard: 'If You've Got It, Rock It!'" *Guardian*, September 13, 2016. TheGuardian.com/fashion/2016/sep/13/lady-with-a-beard-if-youve-got-it-rock-it-guinness-world-records.

Khoo, Isabelle. "5 Reasons Constance Wu Is One Kickass Woman." *HuffPost Canada*, March 22, 2017. HuffPost.com/archive/ca/entry/constance-wu_n_15542770?ncid=fcbklnkcahpmg00000001.

King, Noel. "Trans People 'Have Always Been There,' Says 'Disclosure' Producer Laverne Cox." NPR, July 13, 2020. NPR.org/2020/07/13/889840406/trans -people-have-always-been-there-says-disclosure-producer-laverne-cox.

Koday, Dan. "Samira, Samira, Let Down Your Hair." *InStyle*, November 15, 2015. InStyle. com/beauty/samira-wiley-interview-beauty-lgbt-37-movie.

Kondo, Marie. *The Life-Changing Magic of Tidying Up: The Japanese Art of Decluttering and Organizing*. Berkeley, CA: Ten Speed Press, 2014.

KonMari. "Marie Kondo Interviews Elizabeth Gilbert on Tidying the Mind." Accessed August 13, 2021. KonMari.com/marie-kondo-interviews-elizabeth-gilbert.

Kübler-Ross, Elisabeth, and David Kessler. *Life Lessons: Two Experts on Death & Dying Teach Us about the Mysteries of Life & Living*. New York: Scribner, 2014.

Kuga, Mitchell. "On Writing for the Muses." The Creative Independent, January 27, 2020. TheCreativeIndependent.com/people/astrologer-and-author-chani -nicholas-on-writing-for-the-muses.

Laderer, Ashley. "The State of Our Mental Health: Dr. Joy, Therapy for Black Girls." *Talkspace* (blog), May 19, 2020. Talkspace.com/blog/he-state-of-our-mental -health-dr-joy-harden-bradford.

La Duke, Phil. "Sallie Krawcheck of Ellevest: 'It's Never Too Late to Do What You Were Meant to Do.'" Thrive Global, May 5, 2020. ThriveGlobal.com/stories/sallie -krawcheck-of-ellevest-its-never-too-late-to-do-what-you-were-meant-to-do.

Lane, Carly. "Ming-Na Wen on *Agents of S.H.I.E.L.D.*'s Final Season and the Possibility of Philinda." SYFY, June 12, 2020. SYFY.com/syfywire/ming-na-wen-on-agents -of-shields-final-season-and-the-possibility-of-philinda.

Lewis, Rachel. "Aaron Rose Philip Is Blazing Trails for Disabled, Black, and Trans Talent." *Indie Magazine*, May 4, 2021. Indie-Mag.com/2021/04/aaron-rose-philip-gucci.

Lindsey, Sue. "NASA Pioneer Katherine Johnson Q&A." AARP, February 19, 2018. AARP.org/politics-society/history/info-2018/katherine-johnson-fd.html.

Ludlam, Julia. "20 Brené Brown Quotes That Will Empower You to Be a Courageous Leader." *Country Living*, June 3, 2020. CountryLiving.com/life/inspirational-stories /g32757574/brene-brown-quotes/?slide=8.

"MacArthur 'Genius' and Bestselling Author Angela Duckworth on Perseverance and Conquering Fear." Writing Routines, February 20, 2019. WritingRoutines.com /angela-duckworth-interview.

Maine, D'Arcy. "Serena Williams Shades Body Shamers: 'I've Got Grand Slams to Win.'" ESPN, August 31, 2015. ESPN.com/espnw/athletes-life/the-buzz/story/_/id /13550586/got-grand-slams-win.

Mandy Martini Chihuailaf. "About." Accessed August 13, 2021. M-Martini.com/about.

Manning, Charles. "Nyma Tang on What the Beauty Industry Still Gets Wrong about Dark Skin." Daily Front Row, November 19, 2019. FashionWeekDaily.com /nyma-tang.

March, Bridget. "Life Lessons from Iskra Lawrence." *Harper's Bazaar,* January 29, 2018. HarpersBazaar.com/uk/beauty/mind-body/a15387498/iskra-lawrence-interview.

Mazzo, Lauren. "Jessamyn Stanley Is One Step Closer to Becoming Queen of the Yoga World." *Shape*, April 30, 2021. Shape.com/celebrities/interviews/jessamyn -stanley-adidas-formotion-interview.

McDonough, Lee Chaix. *ACT on Your Business*. 2019.

McNay, Anna. "Shirin Neshat: 'Nothing Is More Powerful Than Human Expression.'" Studio International: Visual Arts, Design and Architecture, April 23, 2015. StudioInternational.com/index.php/shirin-neshat-interview-home-of-my-eyes -yarat-baku-azerbaijan-photography.

McRae, Donald. "PSG's Nadia Nadim: 'I Know the Value of Helping a Person When They Have No Hope.'" *Guardian*, April 27, 2020. TheGuardian.com/football/2020/apr/27/psg-nadia-nadim-football-refugee-reconstructive-surgeon-taliban-denmark.

Mead, Christina. "Before and after the Gold: An Interview with Gabby Douglas." *Life Teen* (blog), accessed August 1, 2021. LifeTeen.com/blog/before-after-gold-an-interview-with-gabby-douglas.

Metz, Chrissy. "*This Is Us*' Chrissy Metz Pens Powerful Letter to Her Teenage Self: 'Stop Comparing Yourself' to Others." *People*, April 18, 2017. People.com/celebrity/chrissy-metz-worlds-most-beautiful-essay.

M.M. LaFleur. "Lisa Lucas's Novel Way to Change the World." April 12, 2019. MMLaFleur.com/mdash/lisa-lucas-interview.

Morris, Alex. "Blake Lively Is 'Awakened': The Actress Talks Sexism in Hollywood and Raising Fearless Daughters." *Glamour*, July 31, 2017. Glamour.com/story/blake-lively-september-2017-cover-interview.

Mosley, Tonya. "Poet Sonya Renee Taylor's Words of Wisdom for the Class of 2020." *Here & Now*. WBUR, May 22, 2020. WBUR.org/hereandnow/2020/05/22/sonya-renee-taylor-graduates.

Muldowney, Katie, Ignacio Torres, and Alexia Valiente. "Transgender Teen and 'I Am Jazz' Star Jazz Jennings on Sharing the Final Steps of Her Transition Journey: Her Gender Confirmation Surgery." *ABC News,* October 15, 2018. ABCNews.go.com/Health/transgender-teen-jazz-star-jazz-jennings-sharing-final/story?id=58513271.

Mullen, Pat. "Tatyana McFadden Goes for Gold in Netflix's Rising Phoenix." *Point of View Magazine,* August 26, 2020. POVMagazine.com/tatyana-mcfadden-rising-phoenix-interview-documentary-netflix.

Murphy, Lauren. "Enya Breaks Her Silence on Fame, Privacy and Music." *Irish Times*, November 13, 2015. IrishTimes.com/life-and-style/people/enya-breaks-her-silence-on-fame-privacy-and-music-1.2428630.

Newcomb, Alyssa. "Kerry Washington: 'Scandal' Star Shares Memories from Her College Years." *ABC News*, May 19, 2013. ABCNews.go.com/Entertainment/kerry-washington-scandal-star-honorary-doctorate-george-washington/story?id=19211377.

Newman-Bremang, Kathleen. "This Conversation with Angela Bassett Will Clear Your Skin, Pay Your Taxes, Water Your Crops, Etc." Refinery29, May 17, 2021. Refinery29.com/en-us/2021/05/10473580/angela-bassett-interview-wellness-aging-beauty-tina-turner.

Nugent, Edie. "CS Interview: Phillipa Soo Talks Hamilton & Playing Leading Lady Eliza." ComingSoon.net, June 30, 2020. ComingSoon.net/movies/features/1140218-cs-interview-phillipa-soo.

Obama, Michelle. "Remarks by the First Lady during Keynote Address at Young African Women Leaders Forum." National Archives and Records Administration, June 22, 2011. ObamaWhiteHouse.archives.gov/the-press-office/2011/06/22/remarks-first-lady-during-keynote-address-young-african-women-leaders-fo.

O'Dowd, Peter, and Allison Hagan. "Jasmine Harrison Is the Youngest Woman to Row Solo across the Ocean." *Here & Now*. WBUR, February 24, 2021. WBUR.org/hereandnow/2021/02/24/jasmine-harrison-solo-row.

On Being Project. "Michelle Alexander—Who We Want to Become: Beyond the New Jim Crow." Accessed August 1, 2021. OnBeing.org/programs/michelle-alexander-who-we-want-to-become-beyond-the-new-jim-crow.

Peppers, Gia. "Jill Scott on New Album 'Woman,' Her Son Jet & Advice for New Artists." *Essence*, December 6, 2020. Essence.com/celebrity/exclusive-jill-scott-new-album-woman-her-son-jet-advice-new-artists.

Powell, Angel. "Breaking Norms on Wheels: An Interview with Jillian Mercado." Adolescent, October 26, 2018. Adolescent.net/a/breaking-norms-on-wheels-an-interview-with-jillian-mercado.

Pridgett, Tamara. "These Indigenous Women Are Defining Wellness for Themselves." *Teen Vogue*. March 10, 2021. TeenVogue.com/story/these-indigenous-women-are-defining-wellness-for-themselves.

Quindlen, Anna. *Being Perfect*. New York: Random House, 2009.

Quinn, Cat. "How Viola Davis Learned to Walk the Red Carpet on *Her* Terms." Refinery29, February 24, 2017. Refinery29.com/en-us/2017/02/142397/viola-davis-natural-hair-makeup-beauty-meaning.

Ramirez, Erika. "Beyonce Takes Fans behind the Scenes on MTV Special." *Billboard*, July 1, 2011. Billboard.com/articles/columns/the-juice/469401/beyonce-takes-fans-behind-the-scenes-on-mtv-special.

Reeves Turner, Alice. "Tokyo 2020: Refugee Olympic Team Swimmer Yusra Mardini Speaks of the Importance of [the Her] Team to the Olympic Games." Eurosport, July 25, 2021. EuroSport.com/swimming/tokyo-2020/2021/tokyo-2020-refugee-olympic-team-swimmer-yusra-mardini-speaks-of-the-importance-of-the-her-team-to-th_sto8438694/story.shtml.

Rhimes, Shonda. *Year of Yes*. New York: Simon & Schuster, 2015.

Rocero, Geena. "Transcript of 'Why I Must Come Out.'" TED. Accessed August 8, 2021. TED.com/talks/geena_rocero_why_i_must_come_out/transcript?language=en.

Roenigk, Alyssa. "Jordyn Wieber Survived Abuse, and Is Now Out to Change Gymnastics Culture." ESPN, April 1, 2021. ESPN.com/olympics/story/_/id/31169775/jordyn-wieber-survived-abuse-now-change-gymnastics-culture.

Rose, Steve. "'Being Black in America Requires Emotional Aerobics': Regina King on 'Powder Keg' Movie *One Night in Miami*." *Guardian*, January 8, 2021. TheGuardian.com/film/2021/jan/08/regina-king-one-night-miami-oscar-winning-beale-street-actor-black-lives-matter.

Ross, Harling. "The One Thing Marie Kondo Regrets Giving Away." Repeller, January 31, 2019. Repeller.com/marie-kondo-interview.

Royal Family. "The Duchess of Cambridge Speaks to Jasmine Harrison on World Record for International Women's Day." YouTube, March 8, 2021. YouTube.com/watch?v=p6OQuImvwGw&t=94s&ab_channel=TheRoyalFamily.

Ruisch, Jeni. "The Interview: Theresa Flores." 614, January 2, 2018. 614now.com/2018/culture/community/the-interview-theresa-flores.

Ruiz, Michelle. "Representative Ilhan Omar on Bringing America Back from the Brink." *Vogue*, January 20, 2021. Vogue.com/article/rep-ilhan-omar-on-the-bringing-america-back-from-the-brink.

Sawyer, Miranda. "Margaret Atwood: 'If You're Going to Speak Truth to Power, Make Sure It's the Truth.'" *Guardian*, September 12, 2020. TheGuardian.com/lifeandstyle/2020/sep/12/margaret-atwood-if-youre-going-to-speak-truth-to-power-make-sure-its-the-truth.

Schnall, Marianne. "Interview with Arianna Huffington on new Work-Life Strategies That Boost Resilience and Prioritize Well-Being During COVID and Beyond." *Forbes*, September 15, 2020. Forbes.com/sites/marianneschnall/2020/09/15/interview-with-arianna-huffington/?sh=958974a114ce.

Schnall, Marianne. "Interview with Dolly Parton on Her Latest Projects, the Power of Love and More." *HuffPost*, November 29, 2016. HuffPost.com/entry/interview-with-dolly-parton-on-her-latest-projects_b_583da37ee4b0bb2962f178cb.

Schnall, Marianne. "Madeleine Albright: An Exclusive Interview." *HuffPost,* December 6, 2017. HuffPost.com/entry/madeleine-albright-an-exc_b_604418.

Schnall, Marianne. "'We Are Entitled To Ambition': Stacey Abrams Talks about Leadership, Change, and Her New Book." *Forbes*, May 22, 2019. Forbes.com/sites /marianneschnall/2019/05/22/we-are-entitled-to-ambition-stacey-abrams-talks -about-leadership-change-and-her-new-book/?sh=226cc49a6ca2.

Schumer, Amy. *The Girl with the Lower Back Tattoo*. New York: Gallery Books, 2017.

Self (blog). "Bola Sokunbi from Clever Girl Finance on Overcoming Discrimination and Building Wealth." March 14, 2019. Self.inc/blog/clever-girl-finance-interview.

Sharf, Zack. "Gabourey Sidibe: 'The Seas Didn't Part for Me' Like They Did for Anna Kendrick after Our Oscar Noms." IndieWire, September 19, 2020. IndieWire.com /2020/09/gabourey-sidibe-compares-life-after-oscar-anna-kendrick-1234587457.

SomeGoodNews. "SGN Graduation with Oprah, Steven Spielberg, Jon Stewart, and Malala (EP. 6)." YouTube, May 3, 2020. YouTube.com/watch?v=IweS2CPSnbI& ab_channel=SomeGoodNews.

Spruill, Tamryn. "Q&A with Skylar Diggins-Smith: 'You Owe It to Yourself to Be the Best Version of Yourself.'" Swish Appeal, May 22, 2020. SwishAppeal.com/wnba/2020 /5/22/21267509/skylar-diggins-smith-bodyarmor-only-you-can-phoenix -mercury-wnba.

Stevens, Matt. "Read Kamala Harris's Vice President-Elect Acceptance Speech." *New York Times*, November 8, 2020. NYTimes.com/article/watch-kamala-harris -speech-video-transcript.html.

Strayed, Cheryl. *Wild: From Lost to Found on the Pacific Crest Trail*. New York: Vintage Books, 2013.

Sutton, Samantha. "Gigi Gorgeous Told a White Lie during Her Forbes 30 under 30 Interview." Coveteur, accessed August 1, 2021. Coveteur.com/2017/11/30/gigi-gorgeous-this-is-everything-documentary.

Tahir, Sabaa. *A Torch Against the Night*. New York: Razorbill, 2016.

Texas Conference for Women. "Exclusive Interview: Lupita Nyong'o on Strength, Success and Feeding Her Soul." May 19, 2017. TXConferenceForWomen.org/exclusive-interview-lupita-nyongo-strength-success-feeding-soul.

The Candidly. "Dr. Alfiee Breland-Noble Wants Us to Talk about Mental Health a Lot More." April 13, 2021. TheCandidly.com/2019/dr-alfiee-breland-noble-qanda-on-mental-health-and-trauma.

Time. "Octavia Spencer's Advice to Graduates: 'The Best Years Are Very Much Ahead of You.'" May 14, 2017. Time.com/4778418/octavia-spencer-kent-state-university-graduation-commencement.

United Nations. "Emma Watson at the HeForShe Campaign 2014—Official UN Video." YouTube, September 22, 2014. YouTube.com/watch?v=gkjW9PZBRfk&ab_channel=UnitedNations.

Vaidya, Rujuta. "'To Be Black in America Is to Be Gaslit Everyday of Your Life': Indya Moore Opens up about Their Journey of Self-Growth." *Vogue India*, October 15, 2020. Vogue.in/fashion/content/to-be-black-in-america-is-to-be-gaslit-everyday-of-your-life-indya-moore-opens-up-about-their-journey-of-self-growth.

Vain, Madison. "Hailee Steinfeld on Haiz EP Interview." EW.com, November 10, 2015. EW.com/article/2015/11/10/hailee-steinfeld-haiz-ep-interview.

Waldman, Katy. "Kathryn Hahn Steals the Show Again." *New Yorker*, March 4, 2021. NewYorker.com/culture/the-new-yorker-interview/kathryn-hahn-steals-the-show-again.

Wellesley College. "Toni Morrison's Commencement Address to the Wellesley College Class of 2004." Accessed August 7, 2021. Wellesley.edu/events/commencement/archives/2004commencement/commencementaddress.

Wendling, Hailey. "We Talk to Philippa Gregory about the Future of Historical Fiction." Culture Whisper, January 5, 2018. CultureWhisper.com/r/books/philippa_gregory_interview/11476.

West, Lindy. *Shrill: Notes from a Loud Woman.* New York: Hachette, 2016.

Wiseman, Eva. "Laverne Cox: 'I Can Be So Hard on Myself.'" *Guardian*, February 14, 2021. TheGuardian.com/film/2021/feb/14/laverne-cox-interview-trailblazing-trans-activist-i-can-be-so-hard-on-myself.

Yamato, Jen, and Tracy Brown. "Why Sandra Oh Considers 'Killing Eve' a 'Transitional' Role." *Los Angeles Times*, May 23, 2021. LATimes.com/entertainment-arts/tv/story/2021-05-23/sandra-oh-killing-eve-the-chair-stop-asian-hate.

Acknowledgments

I want to give a huge thanks to my family. Thank you for always supporting me, especially through this year with all of the challenges that it brought.

To my work colleagues, thank you so much for continuing to support me both at work and in all of my outside pursuits.

Last, many thanks to Kayla Park, Aric Dutelle, Ann Edwards, and the entire team at Callisto Media. It has been wonderful to work with all of you on various projects throughout the past year.

About the Author

BRIANA HOLLIS, LSW, is a self-care coach based in Cleveland, Ohio. She is also the author of the *Self-Care Journal for Young Adults* and the *Self-Esteem Journal*.

When she's not working or writing, she loves spending time with her loved ones, traveling the world, and learning everything there is to know about the latest Marvel movie.

You can connect more with Briana on Instagram @learningtobefreeblog or through her website at LearningToBeFree.com.

CPSIA information can be obtained
at www.ICGtesting.com
Printed in the USA
JSHW051811071221
21038JS00003B/3